BTME

A WONDERFUL VIEW OF THE SEA

sbc

Poetry by Ruth Silcock

MRS. CARMICHAEL

Ruth Silcock

A WONDERFUL
VIEW OF THE SEA

ANVIL PRESS POETRY

Published in 1996
by Anvil Press Poetry Ltd
Neptune House 70 Royal Hill London SE10 8RT

20/11/96

Copyright © Ruth Silcock 1996

This book is published
with financial assistance from
The Arts Council of England

The moral rights of the author have been
asserted in accordance with
the Copyright, Designs and Patents Act 1988

Designed by Anvil
Set in Monotype Plantin Light
Printed and bound in England
by Morganprint (Blackheath) Ltd
Distributed by Password, Manchester

ISBN 0 85646 264 0

A catalogue record for this book
is available from the British Library

ACKNOWLEDGEMENTS

Some of these poems have appeared in *Cyphers*, *Honest Ulsterman*, *London Magazine*, *Poetry Review*, *Rialto*, *Smiths Knoll* and *The Spectator*.

'The Horse' received a special commendation in the National Poetry Competition in 1992.

CONTENTS

46 NURSING HOMES

AMERICAN FRIENDS

(most of whom have, according to others, disappeared)

Where have they gone, my American friends,
Down what manhole, out of what window?
The manner of their vanishing depends
More on some oversight than plan to go.

The El was torn down, and some people went too.
They cleaned up the Bowery, and cleaned up you.

No one said, Let's leave the Village –
Grew tired with Times Square.
No ferries, tunnels, took them –
Paying passengers – elsewhere.

To buy a ticket, or to drive a car,
Is not to disappear.

The sidewalk shows no footprint, the pavement shows no track,
The space between skyscrapers is fresh air, not a crack.
The buildings stand as sound
As if in iron bound
Where no weakness can be found.

In the small rock parks the children play.
Whoever came to watch them, as easily went away.
No one minds if you stay.

East and west, block after block – airports, oceans – nothing
        ends,
New faces come and go through my disappearing friends.

A VISIT TO THE GOLD COAST

This is the Gold Coast, these palaces
Built on Long Island Sound.
Gravel drives, gates and shrubberies
Mark the landward side; but walk round
To the lawns and pools and jetties and private sea.
'Home,' say the family.

English, Moorish, Dutch, Colonial
Mansions on the strand.
A sister liked brick and a brother stucco.
Someone's loving hand
Presented a public library of bound books
To a man of modest looks.

This aunt chose chintz in rose and yellow
To blossom on beds and chairs.
The Gainsborough was a gift. She stands
By a flight of Spanish stairs
Near a nautical cocktail bar of brass and glass,
Where men watch their own ships pass.

A woman walks her dogs. Her raincoat
Is buff, the lawns brilliant green.
Two people plunge in a swimming-pool,
Pink dolphins seen through a screen
Of white sea-mist, that drapes and trails about
Till the golden homes are shut out.

Bells chime and clang through the fog, waves ripple,
A seagull sits on a post.
Paint flakes from the wooden rails of the jetty.
The air is damp, the coast
Is nothing but birds and bells, the jetty, the sea.
People feel alone and free.

Pavilions, palaces, farms and cabins
Line the coast road. Everyone
Has their own dream of home. They like the view
Of the sea in summer, the sun
Scorching, the bodies burning, the bright playground:
In this case, along the Sound.

THE HOUSE BY THE LAKE

'We spent our summers
In a house beside a lake.
How we loved that house.

But people grow up.
It was time to sell the house.
How we loved that house.

Many years later
We went back to see the house.
The house was locked up.

Locked up – in summer!
We peered through all the windows.
Nothing had been changed.

We could see our lamps,
Our same old tables and chairs,
Our books and pictures.

What ailed these owners?
Why didn't they dare to touch
One thing? Anything!

We haven't been back.
They locked our house in summer.
How we loved that house.'

THE WATERY WORLD

Last summer we poled
A punt over smothered weeds,
Grey bubbles rising.

On our pond or mere,
While we leant picking lilies
Long stems sucked at us.

Day-trippers at sea,
Skylarking out, we pulled home
Against wind, wave, tide.

Then the blue ocean,
Flying fish, albatross, spray.
Red and black sunsets.

A picture window.
See the storm strike the harbour.
See white sails floating –

Or a mountain lake,
Bird butterfly boat stopped, blocked
By cliffs of shadow.

TV. I'm watching
Lovers aboard a liner
In dirty weather.

The horizon tilts.
They tilt, and my head goes tilt,
We slope together

On boards that billow,
Ship smashed at by chunks of green,
The long uncoiling

Wet slither of weeds.
I clutch the arm of my chair
By shadowy cliffs.

SLEEPING ON DECK

It was so hot on deck,
Night as thick as blankets,
Air sticky with tar,
Lovers like engines throbbing.

It was so hot on deck
Till the sailors came at dawn
With buckets of salt water
Sluicing us down to the cabins.

Steam rising from each bunk,
Cockroaches on the walls,
Smell of sweat and sick –
G Deck, Inside, Eight Berth –

Forcing us back to the sun
Where we lay all day in a furnace,
Awake all night in a furnace,
Listening to engines throbbing.

THE DESERT SANDS

Landscape in caverns,
A road, an inn, some palm trees
Dug in a sandpit.

Overhead, sand dunes,
Moonlight on peaks, eaves, ridges.
Down here, we breathe sand.

We rush to the inn,
We queue for drinks, snacks, toilets,
Rush back to the bus.

Sand drifts on the road.
We drive past hanging sand cliffs,
Villages, palm trees.

GREENISH

'Green is the colour of the dead.'
'That poem's morbid,' someone said.
'Why green, not grey or white or blue?'
'I do not think the poem true.'
'Corruption in the dead can show
A shiny phosphorescent glow
That's nearly green.' 'We do not know.'

They sat on sofas, chairs and floor,
Five people wedged within the door.
Eva, her cigarette alight,
Sure in her corner, said 'He's right,
The dead are greenish. I have seen
Dead people; greenish; not quite green.'
Greenish dead people can be found
In brownish clothes upon the ground.
The snow is whitish where they lie,
And reddish-eyed, the mourners cry.
'The poet's nearly right,' she said.
'Greenish, the colour of the dead.'

THE MOTOR-BIKE

Travelling somewhere,
Yawning from boredom, almost glum,
Driving with dull care
Through evening traffic rushing home –
I saw a boy spring in the air,
Spin, twist and float,
Dance overhead in thick black leather coat,
Hover in helmet, gloves, fall down,
Screams rising from his throat.

'My bike,' he was screaming,
Rolling in traffic, curled to the ground,
Cuddling the gleaming
Broken black motor-bike he'd found.
Friends gathered, stooped,
Crouched in the road to make a ring.
A flock of birds settled on everything.
We could not drive away from the sound,
His weeping in the evening.

FIRE AT HEADINGTON CREMATORIUM

Over Oxfordshire
Clouds of darkness come.
    What's on fire?
The crematorium.

Ambulance, police
Have been telephoned.
    Obsequies
Cannot be postponed.

While the Fire Brigade
Rush to fight the blaze,
    Undismayed
The congregation prays.

The funeral begins
(The organist is late –
    Fire engines
Block the entrance gate).

Hymns and flames arise,
Spouts of water stream.
    In the skies
Rainbows leap and steam.

Dust dissolves in dust,
Ashes quench in ash,
    Caskets rust,
Urn and altar splash.

Firefighters relax,
Undertakers smile,
    Hearse, hose, axe
Idle for a while.

Priests in robes, police,
Mourners stroll about,
Rest in peace
Now the fire is out.

MISHEARD CONVERSATION

He said, 'Have you seen red cows
On the hillside, over there,
Across the white valley, amongst the trees,
On the steepest slope?
They don't seem to mind the gulf. They come to browse.'

'Yes,' she said, 'I saw a red car
At the foot of the valley, where
It had crashed in the stream. The top road must freeze
As slippery as soap,
With no fence or wall or bank to be a bar.'

'I wouldn't like,' he said, 'to come down
Such a steep hill. The slide
To me would be unstoppable: but watch those cows,
Hungry I suppose,
Picking their delicate way, they don't slither or drown.'

'The car was red. Fire and rust
Ate it. The driver must have died
Speeding, or late, or beginning to drowse.
In frozen snows
He'd skid, smash down through trees, burn, drown. Now he's
        just

Another valley memory. Brave
Or foolish or unlucky. The place
Is haunted. Even modern ghosts abound.'
'Red cows,' he said,
'Are admirable, absurd. The grass they crave

Is on the perpendicular, yet
Carefully they descend, with bovine grace,
Safely through trees and bracken, till they've found
Food and are fed.'
Pleased with the round red cows, their hearing met.

AFTERNOON TEA WITH A
RETIRED HISTORY TEACHER

An upstairs flat, quite near the sea.
A bed, a table, two armchairs.
A window, and outside, a tree.

The green tree blocks the light, and there's
A shadow on your chair. You fade
To silence or to sleep. It scares

Me wide awake, to see the shade
Of summer leaves, and not see you,
As if you've gone already, made

Farewells I didn't hear, slipped through
The sliding leaves, and left a space,
An empty chair I'm talking to.

I peer through air to find your face.
A trick of light sits in your place.

★

And there you are, within your chair.
I've made you out, recovered you,
Your body bent for sleep, your hair

Cut like a child's. You rise to view
In the green suit you always wore.
You blink, sit up straight, ask me to

Move my chair closer than before.
We study each other by twilight.
I'm wrong, by forty years or more,

Your hair's not straight and grey, it's white,
Thin, waved. You wear a dress. Your face
Doubts at me also. Dulled eyesight

Muddled by tricks of shade and space
Has put past bodies in our place.

★

An upstairs flat (younger than me),
Two armchairs (filled with blocked-out light),
A tree that grows and dies, a sea

That eats the town, while two polite
Changed people, strangers, smile and hand
A plate of biscuits and recite

Old jokes, old anecdotes, to stand
As proof, those past times were quite true.
Perched up in air, we share that land

Of constant history. We too
Can play some tricks on time and space
And win some wars, though briefly. – You

Push the green shadows from your face.
I will write down the date and place.

16.8.81
Bexhill-on-Sea

BACK WARDS

Patients are used instead of paint
To rest the eye from ruling lines
Of corridors and wards.

In silent rows the patients sit
With aprons, folded arms, and rock,
Bend over and cradle their dreams.

SIX VIEWS OF COUSINS IN SCOTLAND

Friends seemed to speak of visits to cousins in Scotland, but it later
turned out that these cousins' existence was in my misapprehension.

I   DISTANT COUSINS

I thought they said Glencoe, or Rannoch Moor –
Two travellers in their car, driving uphill
To reach the far-off cottage, sunlit door,
And wait with smiles and cakes and flowers, until
The door opens on darkness. – 'Mother's ill.
You can't come in, you can't have tea today,'
Their cousin says. 'No, you can't help, it will
Be best if you forget us.' Hair now grey,
Dress drab, voice dull, eyes desperate. They say
Of course they understand, of course they'll go
And leave their cousins in peace, and turn away
Unwelcome down the hillside, sad and slow
Through the brown heather, wanting towns and tea.
– The couple in the cottage trouble me.

2   THIS TIME LAST YEAR

Here is the cottage: small and white and square.
Here are the women: middle-aged and old.
The elder by the fireside in her chair,
The younger busy bustling as she's told –
Now sweep the floor, now polish brass, now hold
A skein of wool, or plump up cushions, bring
More coals, shake rugs, shut doors, it may turn cold.
Visitors are expected. Everything
Is tidy, clean and cheerful, welcoming.
Flowers in the windows, best cups on the tray.
Here come the distant cousins, travelling
Over the moors to meet them, and today
Will be so happy, let's all meet next year –
Glencoe or Rannoch – but the plan is clear.

3   THIS TIME THIS YEAR

So this is Scotland on a summer's day.
The flash and sparkle of a thousand cars.
Tourists stare out from every parking bay
At drifts of snow-white Kleenex, crystal spars
Of brilliant fractured windscreens, bottles, jars
All dazzling in the heather. Silly sheep
Chew chips and crisps and foil from chocolate bars.
Flies buzz and radios hum and people sleep.
Scotland is wild and picturesque and cheap
For picnics on the moor, tents in the glen.
We all have tartan blood, and come to keep
Appointments with our history again.
A jaunt in summer to a festive tea.
Here's the dear cottage that we came to see.

4   EVENING

The shadow on the sofa is the mother.
The daughter is the image by the door.
I never heard of father, husband, brother –
Hated perhaps, or vanished in some war –
Just these two women handcuffed on the moor,
One lying down in darkness, one upright,
A granite post with rounded mouth to pour
Her silent shrieking bellows day and night,
A cow, an owl, a pig, a beast in flight. –
The shadow shifts, the granite gives, the ghost
That walked across their graves gave them a fright.
Now comes the pleasant time they love the most.
Comfort and warmth and cards. The windows shine
Yellow across the moor. The night is fine.

5   HELP MAY BE AT HAND

I sit with my directory and dream:
How do such people manage far away?
Have they Home Helps? And Meals-on-Wheels? A scheme
For Granny-sitting volunteers? Do they
Get help with transport (is there transport?), pay
For spectacles and teeth and feet? Who calls?
Where is the nearest chemist? What delay
In finding beds (what beds?) if mother falls?
(The dark and lonely cottage. Mother crawls
Over the floor. There is no telephone.)
Soon men will come with bath aids, rails for walls
And walking-frames and bells. Now never alone.
– Have you heard any news about those two?
Still desperate within that lovely view?

6   SCOTLAND FAREWELL

Cousins in Scotland? Desperate? With a view?
– They don't know what I mean. It's my mistake.
Moorland and glen and heather are all true,
The rest all wrong. But how can I forsake
Those women in my mind? How can I shake
Their dust off me, and shove them out, and say
Please leave me as you came, since you are fake?
For a whole year I followed their harsh way,
Worse than my friends', or any known – and they
Accompanied my days. I cared for them.
Things could improve. They might have moved. They may
Be happier now. They don't exist. They stem
From half-heard words, from gaps and gulfs, from air.
Their far white house is empty. Real friends near.

BOOKS

'The best ones are upstairs, the precious books.'
Let's follow. Here's adventure. Poor old boy. –
Such creaky, greasy, murky stairs to lead
To treasure trove. 'My snug. Sorry it looks
Untidy.' Stench and squalor. 'I employ
My time with study. Read, sleep eat and read.'
Camp-bed unmade, oil fire, a string and hooks
For pans and cloths and clothes. Bucket. 'Enjoy
My books.' His towers and groves. 'My books.' – Our need
To panic from this cavern where he cooks,
Sleeps, breathes and urinates, and will destroy
Civilization. Great books must be freed.
'My temple.' Rotting in the warm rank air.
'You desecrate,' he says. 'Get out of here.'

'PENALTY KICK FOR PARKING ON YELLOW LINE'

Headline in the Observer

'I parked my car on a yellow line.
Policemen told me to move it away.
(They say the right to complain is mine.)

– I was sorry, we argued, they swore. I was fine
Till they grabbed my neck, hit me and punched me that day
I parked my car on a yellow line.

Two police officers chose to combine,
Arrest, drive me off, call me shitface. I lay
(They say the right to complain is mine)

In the road outside Hounslow Police Station, nine
Or ten steps from the door. They are right when they say
I parked my car on a yellow line,

So they kick me between my legs, and decline
To fetch doctor or water, condemn me to stay
(They say the right to complain is mine)

Two hours, sick with pain, very swollen, a sign
Of a testicle broken. The fine that I pay.
I parked my car on a yellow line.
(They say the right to complain is mine.)'

'REMEMBER ME – ' II

'Remember me – '
She said, and he
Said 'Yes of course I will.
So young, such fun
For everyone
Except when you are ill.'

'Remember me – '
She said, and he
Said 'Yes of course I do.
Friend, mother, wife,
So kind, such life.
We all feel loved by you.'

'Remember me –
Please come – ' and he
Remembered, couldn't go.
To see her changed,
Pale, frail, deranged –
It would upset him so.

CARRYING ON THE MISSION

Such a serious man who likes playing the clown,
Standing At Ease in a military way
With a baleful look and a beetling frown

And black Sunday suit and stiff collar and grey
Hard Homburg hat worn side to side
('Napoleon broods on his fate today')

In a garden of palm trees, bamboos, wide
Half-cropped lawn, pots, blocks of stone,
Each flower cherished and staked and tied

By his wife (in another picture) now gone.
– He is ending his days by this northern sea.
If it weren't for her he would be alone

But outside his sitting-room window he
Sees a smooth green lawn and a small earth bed
And the soul of his wife in a yellow rose tree.

He introduces his wife who is dead.
A bowl of her roses sweetens the room.
In their garden of palm, what a life they'd led,

Jokes, friends, weddings, the guest-house, the groom
And bride clasped in dark. The river, the town,
Their mission, now his. How her flowers must bloom.

MRS. BROWNE COULD NOW
BE SIXTY-FIVE

A hospital in London. A long ward.
A Mrs. Browne asleep within a bay.
'Wake her,' the Staff Nurse tells me. 'Wake,' I say
Softly, then louder. Touch her, shake her hard.
A shame to wake her, sleeping peacefully.
'Nonsense,' says Staff Nurse. 'Here's her cup of tea.'

Pink as a baby, curling hair, white lids,
Blue flowers on her nightdress. Fast asleep.
Ladies in beds surround us. 'Poke her. Keep
Talking, tell her she's won the pools, the kids
Are crying for her, tall dark handsome men
Are queueing up to kiss her.' And again

I say her name and take her hand and touch
Her forehead, lift her lids. Her eyes are blue.
She's breathing deeply. Seize her shoulders. Who
Could sleep through this absurd attack, so much
Alarm, bells ringing, rousing in this bay
Of one long quiet ward? 'Wake up!' we say.

So peaceful Mrs. Browne was summoned back
To walk about our world again, although
She'd wanted rest, a pillowed head, a slow
Smother of warmth and blankets, stretched out, slack
And heavy. No more waking. – Not our brave
Loud shouts of rescue, thrill and skill to save.

JAPANESE LANDSCAPE PRINTS

by Hokusai and Hiroshige

White foxes gather
Under a bare tree. Starlight.
Here come blue foxes.

★

The fish eagle swoops
On Mount Fuji, snowfields, sea
And one lobster-pot.

★

Three pines and three pines.
Our three pines and our picnic.
Far three pines and dark.

★

Blue waves leap upward,
Froth blossoms on the mountain,
Treetop, boat and bay.

★

Our sandy path led
To a view of pale water,
Pale mountain, pale sky.

★

Even in winter,
With snow on homes, hills, jetty,
Some people must work.

★

Ladies in a park,
Chattering in the twilight,
Hooded and shrouded.

★

Trust our bridge of ropes
Crossing red mountain gorges.
Men haul, baskets swing.

★

Snow blossom falling
On house and hill and river.
Boatman, time for home.

★

Sandbanks and rivers.
Porters strip off, drag baggage,
Hoist the brown monks, wade.

★

Straw hats, parasols,
Straw coats, bare legs and sandals,
We rush through rainstorms.

★

Neat houses, fences,
Tired horses, busy people
And pink Mount Fuji.

★

Snowflakes and forest.
Downhill goes the white rider,
Uphill the village.

LOST AND FOUND

'Some cousins have a farm. Our family
Always spend August there. One red-hot day
We walked through dusty fields till we could see
Treetops, a wooded valley, and a way
Down to a stream, rocks, waterfall. "Let's play!"
Our son said, lost in undergrowth and shade
And found, not drowned, at bedtime. We were so afraid.'

Another time another family sat
All afternoon on a churchyard bench, and gazed
Down terraces of graves to forests that
Blurred into blue like water, dazed and hazed
By space and summer. My mother stood, amazed
– To follow the steep path down to the deepest wood
And be lost and afraid and call and be found, like safe
        childhood?

I lost two hours last month, looking for tea,
Driving the crisscross roads, once well-known way –
Rest Home and forest, cream tea and forest, where we
Circled the afternoons – pubs, trees, café,
Horses and birds and forest. Storm. Trees lay
Smashed up and battered. Daylight everywhere.
No paths, no dark, just fields, but lost, not found, and fear.

If I sit still, or in the night, the trees
Grow tall and dark and silent. I make out
This person ahead, walking intently. She's
So sure to find the well of the woods. – If I shout
She might look up, she might look back, might doubt
Direction in the forest, call my name.
How far she's gone. What crowds in the woods. I can hear
        a child's game.

CRESSEID BLAMES THE GODS

'I am so sad,'
Said poor Cresseid,
'Since Diomede
Has made me bad
I've lost the looks I had.

He tired of me,
Sent me from home,
And so I've come
For company
And food, to lechery.

Once flower of May,
I lay in pride
By Troilus' side
Till led away.
I did not mean to stray.

I'm not to blame,
The gods did this,
They promised bliss,
Great love, great fame.
But all my fame is shame.

Wretched Cresseid.
I knelt to chide
False gods who lied
And they agreed
Vengeance on my misdeed.

They seized my hair,
They blotched my face,
Deformed my grace,
Blurred my soft stare,
Sent scabs and rags and care.

Unclean, outcast,
I beg for bread.
The others said
Sir Troilus passed –
Wept, gave, but went at last.

★

A leper lies
By the roadside,
A cloth to hide
Her face and eyes,
And begs. One day she dies.

'SUMMER LIGHTNING'

A painting by Walter Sickert, who said:
'Paint pictures with something happening in them.'

A picture where something happens? A young woman
                                                    stands
With her back to a stile, with her head half-turning,
                                            her hands
Active and pale, one a bird's foot, balanced
                                        and touching
The broad wooden crossbar (loose in its socket),
                                        one clutching
Close into her side a scarf or a handkerchief.
                                        Pain?
Dread? A child stirring? Not pleasure. A weapon?
                                    – The lane
Goes over the hill between oak tree and cliff-top,
                                        but she
Has her right ear tuned to a man inland.
                                    He can't see
Her face (as we can) because of her bonnet.
                                    Winds blow
The dark ribbons seaward. Two trees lean to seaward,
                                    and show
A frenzy of branches and leaves. Does the man have
                                a gun?
Or a cloak on his shoulder? The woman's uncertain,
                                may run
Though her gown is so full and so heavy, and streaked
                                by the light
That shines on the man framed by trees. All the background
                                seems white,
All the shade in the foreground. Don't trust the broad stile,
                                mouldered post.
You must run. Summer lightning is playing with shadows
                                and ghost.

BRUGES

Here we are in Bruges.
We are in a large high room.
We can sit all day in the window.
We can see a canal from the window.

Here are two adults, fond,
And here is their little white dog
Which leaps for a piece of string
From a bouncing balloon on the ceiling.

Here is a bored child
Leaning out of a window.
Here is a priest. His black hat
Has breadcrumbs dropped in the brim.

Here are boats and bridges,
Bells and churches and paintings,
Madonnas and martyrs, a judge
Being flayed like a peeled banana.

Here are noises at night,
Two fond adults in trouble,
One child under the bedclothes,
One sad adult at breakfast.

'Here is the ward.' Lines of beds
Filled by women in nighties with babies.
Here is the last bed. A woman
In a nightie without a baby.

Bruges is a market town
Famed for its thrice-consumed belfry,
Madonnas with babies, and martyrs,
And people peeled like bananas.

A DRINK BEFORE LUNCH

'A drink before lunch?' asks a neighbour. Of course they will
    go,
Flattered and flurried and boastful. 'Bring friends.' They can
    show
Their guests from the town that they too mix with glamour,
    wealth, fame.
Five eager people are walking towards a great name.

There are wicker chairs, deckchairs, a blanket, a lawn and
    a stream.
Silent helpers are opening bottles. Ice clinks. Glasses gleam.
The queen, Peggy Gibbons, is teasing a one-legged friend
Who smiles, asks for more. Is she honoured? Or does she
    depend

On her frizzy-haired, pudgy tormentor? The locals feel shame,
Except for a kindly old lady who studies the game
And nods, while the queen tells her court of her lovers, such
    bores,
'And the worst bore,' she tells the old lady, 'was Gerald, once
    yours.'

The queen and her court think it funny. The friend with one leg
Splits her sides, though the guests and the locals (including old
    Meg,
White-haired, soft-hearted, whose husband was Gerald, the
    bore)
Are doubting their ears. Meg's two children would head for the
    door

If they weren't in a garden with flowers, rockery, stream –
This is drinks before lunch on a Sunday, in England, our
    dream.
They had wanted their guests to enjoy the exotic, bizarre,
Transatlantic new neighbour who's recently gone far too far.

Did their white-headed mother just scream, her soul skinned
  for a joke?
(Peggy Gibbons can never resist a dig, punch or poke.)
The children are upright. They glower. No one laughs now.
Peggy Gibbons wants Meg for a mother. She loves her, so how

Could she hurt her? 'I'm not hurt!' Meg comforts poor Peggy,
  sad child,
And they hug, true affection, while Peggy's companions go wild
And applaud and fill glasses. Meg's children, dishonoured and
  dumb,
Hang their heads. Peggy's sorry. The visitors ('Why did we
  come?')

Talk of trains. The stream twinkles. Oh England should be safe
  and dull.
Poor Peggy. Poor children. Poor Gerald. Meg laughs in the lull.

A ROSY PINK AND APPLE GREEN MILK JUG

Pink. And cream and green. Pink. Pink.
Green candlewick upon the toilet seat.
Cream wallpaper with roses, raspberry pink
Bedspread, pink satin cushions, cream mat. Chink
Through cherry curtains to the railway. – Drink
Warm tea downstairs, pale green and palest pink
Bone china with white rims. Her white shoes, pink
Laces. Grey knitting-needles, white socks, treat
For some starved foreign child. Not in this street!
(Their bicycles and bells!) More tea. Drink. Think.
A visit to the toilet. Green soap. Brown
Sliding screen door, not soundproof. Hear the clink
Of china cups. Pink plastic bowl, steel sink
Three steps away. Steep stairs. Sleep well. Two pink
Soft towels (but how to close the bathroom door?)
(And how to close the bedroom door?). Cream sheet,
Cold bed. Cold night. Short corridor. A snore
Growling amongst the roses, grunting. Brink
Of nightmare. Dawn. Breakfast – her photos. Floor
Cream, white and pink – her birthday cards. Kneel down.
Stand up. Pack. Pay. Her forehead grey, grey frown.
Jug broken in the sink. Cracked green. Smashed pink.

MR. AND MRS. SMITH

Her name shall be Mrs. Smith.
She has come to complain of her husband.
She sits amongst thirty-odd patients.
She seems the most eager and keen.

Her black coat is musty and greasy,
Her black hat is drooping and greasy,
Her grey face has black in the creases,
Her black eyes are eager and keen.

Her name is now called. Mrs. Smith
Brings her shiny black bag and sits down.
She is solid and heavy and smelly.
She has come to complain about death.

Mrs. Smith is afraid of her husband.
Her husband is plotting to kill her.
Her husband is trying to poison
Mrs. Smith, as if she were a rat.

His name shall be Mr. Smith.
He is skinny and creaky and watchful.
His jacket is threadbare and shiny,
His fingernails bitten and black.

He is eager to tell us his tale.
He came here this morning on purpose.
His wife, wicked woman, hates him.
She will poison him just like a rat.

Mr. and Mrs. Smith
Both left their home this morning.
The ambulance rushed their two bodies
Here to the hospital. Death

Waits by Mrs. Smith's bed.
She is clean, in a hospital nightgown.
Mr. Smith, clean in a nightshirt,
Also sees death by his bed.

Mr. and Mrs. Smith
Are well, and are both going home
To shut their front door and sit down
And wait, side by side by the fire.

SCHOOL RULES

Miss Opel had a big red face,
Big round blue eyes, black frizzy hair.
The new girls liked her best –
The merriest teacher in the place,
The warmest breast.

Miss Brannigan was thin and pale,
Her nose was long, her voice was flat.
Girls often made her cry
And laughed, to see a teacher quail –
Poor thing, so shy.

The school's strict rules did not allow
Swearing or smoking, meeting men,
Litter, or soft armchairs,
Sex talk (particularly how),
Or girls in pairs.

Two girls must not hold hands or kiss,
Two girls must not share bath or bed,
Such girls would have to go.
But all girls also love, a bliss
Girls shouldn't know.

– All girls are also savage. Poor
Miss Brannigan wept all night through.
Miss Opel heard her tears.
Miss Opel opened wide her door
To comfort fears.

Miss Brannigan forgets to grieve,
Two happy friends hold hands and kiss.
A rule is broken – Twang!
Two sinners, bad examples, leave.
A door goes clang.

GREAT UNCLE STANFORD

Great Aunt Alice was kind, her sister Edith had brains,
But young Great Uncle Stanford devoted himself to trains.

Great Aunt Nancy was wise, her sister Ada was fun,
But good Great Uncle Stanford gave pleasure to everyone.

Scrubbed and brushed and polished, always with hat and cane,
He strolled to the station daily to ride on the Underground
      train.

In his topper or summertime boater he queued as anyone
      might,
Requesting a single ticket and sauntering into night.

With his cane tucked under his armpit, his sparkling shoes
      on his feet,
He strode down the escalator like any young man from
      the street.

His choice was the Inner Circle, the train that goes round
      and round,
The train that Great Uncle Stanford loved best on the
      Underground.

Deep in the bowels of London, far below bustle and bus,
Grave Great Uncle Stanford boarded his train without fuss.

He found a quiet corner, he settled at ease in his seat,
He checked his cuffs and his cuff-links, everything clean
      and neat,

He removed a glove to examine his fingernails, winking,
      pink,
Then shook out *The Times* like a shotgun: a gentleman ready
      to think.

The trains in the Inner Circle go round and round and round,
And a well-dressed fellow called Stanford revolves on the
    Underground.

Who can he be, this fellow, this ornament to the Line?
Why! It's Great Uncle Stanford! Exemplary, benign.

THE REVELLERS

Full moon tonight, a picnic, dancing, drinking,
A crowded hall, a service, music playing,
Then the green woodland, summer, time for straying.

At nine o'clock the revellers go, arms linking,
Bright coloured clothes and shining hair, grass swaying,
They meet six bands with banners, children straying.

The hall is full. The food has gone. There's clinking
From Guinness, Harp and Coke cans. Tempers fraying.
Boys besiege girls in toilets, hands are straying.

A Saturnalia in wet woods. Drink sinking
Slowly and coldly from the blood, hounds baying
Over the hill. One lost man drowned while straying.

'And was it good?' At breakfast-time, much thinking,
Heads clasped in hands and stomach-aches and praying
And longing for full moon next year, more straying.

THE ROOM IN THE TOWER

from the story by E. F. Benson

'Jack will show you to your room.
You have been given the room in the tower.'
A dark red house, oppressive gloom,
Tea on the lawn, a heavy shower.

'You have been given the room in the tower.'
Mrs. Stone's voice is always the same.
Tea on the lawn, a heavy shower.
– I was sixteen when this dream first came.

Mrs. Stone's voice is always the same.
I follow her son through the oak-panelled hall.
– I was sixteen when this dream first came.
The view of the garden, the gate in the wall.

I follow her son through the oak-panelled hall.
There's the staircase with corners and then, what I dread,
The view of the garden, the gate in the wall,
From the crimson room with two portraits, a bed.

There's the staircase with corners and then, what I dread
(Fifteen years of this dream and today it is true),
From the crimson room with two portraits, a bed,
I have lawn, wall and gate and her gravestone to view.

(Fifteen years of this dream and today it is true!)
Her tomb glimmers grey through the rough grass and weeds.
I have lawn, wall and gate and her gravestone to view
From the room in the tower where one portrait bleeds.

Her tomb glimmers grey through the rough grass and weeds.
I banish the portrait. It comes back by night
To my room in the tower – her portrait that bleeds!
– By my bed, Mrs. Stone, in the thunderstorm's light!

I banished her portrait. It came back by night.
'I've been long waiting you, I knew you would come.'
– By my bed, Mrs. Stone, in the thunderstorm's light!
I strike her, she falls, I escape, I am home!

'I've been long waiting you, I knew you would come.'
A dark red house? Oppressive gloom?
But I struck her, she fell, I escaped, I am home?
'Jack will show you to your room.'

ONE AFTERNOON A NURSEMAID . . .

One afternoon a nursemaid
Rushed in, Come Quick! the ceiling
Of Room Number Six has fallen
On baby Vanessa.

The grown-ups rushed out, saying
Behave, please play, dear children,
And found Vanessa sleeping,
Surrounded by ceiling.

Next day they let us visit
Empty Room Six, still dusty.
We looked up into Room Seven,
At pictures and lampshades.

The door of Room Number Seven
Was padlocked fast, forbidden,
Though yesterday wide open
For people to enter.

Suppose a person were walking
On a floor that fell down? Edges
Would be the only answer,
And windows and chimneys.

You could cling to the rim of the bedroom
By grate, mantelpiece, curtain,
Hand over hand, or stand frozen
Flat as wallpaper,

Knees jammed hard into corners,
Shoes placed sideways on inches
Of skirting, beading, boarding
Over Vanessa

Far off in her cot and blankets,
Down there amongst hunks of plaster,
Lino and basins and lockers,
Sleeping so soundly.

FREEDOM – THE SOLDIER

This chap long long ago at last was freed
From years and years in prison. He'd been wounded
And partly healed and sent home early, travelled
To find his wife at work with fifty children.

We watched the soldier walking up our drive,
Our hero who had fought for us and freedom.
We waved our flags to show him our proud welcome,
We'd made a bowered nest for him and his wife.

This silent khaki fellow stood in our Home
And held his wife and ate with us and later
They went down to their garnished room together.
– His wife still writes. His wounds don't seem to heal.

FREEDOM – THE CHILDREN

'We're worried about the children.
They race round the field in the evening
As if they were wild things, crazy
Or sickening for something.
Why do they play the fool
The minute they come out of school?

How can we help the children?
Is it the food we give them?
They're not bad children, lazy
Or glum. We forgive them,
But why do they race in the evening,
Silly and strange and leaping?'

A HOUSING PROBLEM

Pale thin Paul
Is nearly twenty years old.
His mother keeps bringing him here.
He's a trouble to his mother.

Paul's mother is plump,
Her cheeks are red, and her hair,
And she likes a life of fun.
Paul's a bad boy to his mother.

Silent sallow Paul
Likes to be left alone.
His voices don't leave him alone
But say, hit someone or other.

Paul and his mother share,
They share a room with each other,
They share their food and their bed
And a chamber-pot together.

Paul is no trouble here
But at home he troubles his mother,
His voices trouble him
And he has to hit someone or other.

A FAVOURITE GAME

We finish dinner,
We don't sit talking,
No drinks, no smoking,
Just games.

We like the knife game.
Spin!

A whizzing knife
On a smooth white cloth
Is slowing down,
And pointing.

Is it pointing at me?
Or pointing at you?
No, it's only a knife,
Just pointing.

We play the game,
Time after time,
And always feel sorry
For George.

ON NOT KNOCKING ON WALTER DE LA MARE'S DOOR WHEN I WAS SIXTEEN YEARS OLD

Suppose when I stood in the rain,
Suppose I had opened the gate,
Suppose I had walked down the drive,
Suppose that I hadn't been late,
Suppose that I knocked on your door,
Suppose you had been inside,
Suppose that you hadn't been busy or tired
Or otherwise occupied,
So suppose that you opened the door
To a soaking wet girl in a mac,
Suppose that she hadn't been scarlet and panting
And wishing that she could turn back –
Suppose she had dripped on your rug,
Suppose that she gave you a cold,
Suppose that she hadn't looked terribly young
While you felt terribly old?
Suppose we had sat down to talk
And talked for an hour or more,
You wouldn't have written later, Alas,
Why didn't you knock on my door?

SOMETHING OF HIMSELF

from Rudyard Kipling

Though it wasn't part of his blood
He met it more early than late,
He had long arrears to make good,
He was five when he learnt to hate.
In a Desolate House by the coast,
He studied how best to hate.

He tried not to show he was moved,
He was icy-willing to wait,
He counted the score and proved
That he was right to hate.
Though the ones he loved the most
Mustn't know how he could hate.

His voice was even and low,
His peering eyes saw straight,
There were only some lies to show
When he began to hate,
When his parents sailed away
And abandoned him to hate.

He said it wasn't the crowd
Who preached it, nor yet the State,
And nobody spoke it aloud,
But wasn't he right to hate
When his sister was praised all day
And left him alone with hate?

It wasn't suddenly bred,
It wouldn't swiftly abate,
There were chilling years ahead,
But his Time could count from the date
He had plotted and planned to destroy
Aunty Rosa and Harry with hate –
When rustles and shades made a boy
Frightened of too much hate.

Why should an old man choose
Plain Miss Mary Postgate,
Companion and nursemaid; why use
A middle-aged woman to state
His anguish? His thrill to lose
His terror, and kill with his hate.

STORIES OF CHINA

Stories of China, of warlords and emperors, dragons and
     demons,
Journeys by river-boat, rickshaw and mule-train or wheeled in
a barrow
(Mother and everyone crouched under coolie hats hiding
     from hornets),
Nuggets of gold to be grated and weighed when you paid for
     your lodging,
Temples with courtyards and gingko trees, lizards, a
     Mandarin peeling
Skin from a peach with his long pointed fingernail sharp as
     a blade.
Centuries, dynasties, tiny feet bandaged up, scholars and
     hermits,
Criminals kneeling down having their heads chopped off
     while you went shopping.
Father was building a college with doorways that baffled
     the devil.
Mother was teaching but never found fault or the girls would
     lose face and
Eat flower of loneliness, lie on their beds and then turn to
     the wall and
Die, poor girls, said my mother so sadly, now glad to go
     home.
– Bridges that swung over gorges where brigands stood
     waiting to shoot us.
Chinese love babies and my sister luckily played with the baby
Brigand, both laughing, so everyone laughed. Then the
     Yangtse; sedan chairs,
Long lines of nappies strung out like white banners; the *amah*,
     grief-stricken,
Running and waving as we sailed to England – our new nurse
     a spy!

PARENTS

Trebitsch Lincoln, father
as well as spy,
travelled by sea to England
to say goodbye
to his son, about to be hanged.
'What a kind old boy,' we thought,
when he stayed with our child at each port,
being banished from land.

A MORNING'S WORK AT TROUTBECK

Cows and calves and sheep with their lambs are running
Down the meadow, hurtling and shoving, dashing
Through the gateway, speeding to reach the corner
Close by the roadside.

Moments later cows (though not sheep) are rushing
Twenty yards away, where they stop and stand and
Slowly turn to file through the gate, then calmly
Climb up the meadow.

Sheep and lambs have scattered on slope and valley,
Cows and calves have vanished, have left their pasture,
Empty fields and – suddenly cows, like magic,
Fill the far meadow!

THE WALL

A baby keeps crying,
It never stops crying
Inside the wall.

It keeps on crying,
Day and night, crying
Inside the wall.

A mother says
She lost her baby,
Now nowhere at all,

Not in the sitting-room,
Not in the bedroom.
Did we hear a call

From a baby crying,
Crying, crying
Inside the wall?

A CHILD CARRIED OUT
TO SEA BY A WAVE

She is playing on the beach,
Inside a tunnel.
The blue glass ceiling shatters,
Sand sucks her feet.
She is wrapped and bundled, hurtled
Past brown breakwaters
Where roaring crams her ears
And head over heels
She plunges salty mountains,
Up to more blue sky.

A GREAT MAN SAYS GOODBYE

A great man is dying,
His family and friends are sitting waiting,
They wait on rows of chairs to say goodbye.

The great man, near dying,
Has begged his friends and family to gather
Their warmth of eighty years outside his door.

His old friends, his best friends,
Have come from far and near, from bed and wheelchair,
Have been collected, shepherded, impressed.

His widow, his orphans,
His ancient girlfriends, secretaries, agent
Stand bunched for comfort, greet the Press, feel cold.

The great man, for dying,
Has chosen a small cubby-hole or lean-to,
A storage shed beyond his workroom door

To lie like a statue
Under three army blankets, greatcoat, muffler,
His old camp-bed flanked by two canvas chairs.

He signals his agent.
The agent beckons two by two, a Noah's Ark.
The visitors line up outside death's door

To enter, each ducking
The cobwebs of the cubby-hole, to settle.
Five minutes each on canvas camping chairs.

The great man is blessing
His oldest friends who hold his hands and kiss him
On cheeks or lips, and wipe their eyes, crack jokes.

The great man is weary,
He waves a last goodbye to friends and girlfriends
Who wave and close his workroom door and go.

His widow, his orphans,
Now gather round their great man in his outhouse
To tuck him up in army blankets, coat.

POOR ARNOLD

'Poor Arnold,' said our mother and grandfather and
    grandmother,
'Poor Arnold,' said his sisters and 'Poor Arnold,' said one
    brother.
Close kin and far connections, girlfriends and wives, lament
'He had a touch of genius – artistic temperament –
Yet ended up a failure.' A failure? When they add
(Especially if they're female) 'he made many women glad.'
Their voices go quite soft and low, their cheeks turn pink,
    eyes bright,
As they fondly say 'dear Arnold' when recounting past
    delight.
All waitresses adored him, all hostesses would press
Fresh invitations – 'Friday? Nine? More soup? More wine?'
    'Why yes!'
While gentlemen with tapping feet and rapping fingers gave
Their grave pronouncement: 'Ladies' man,' and grudgingly,
    'but brave.'
Poor Arnold – short of cash again. Poor Arnold – cause of
    woe.
He sighed then died for one last bride – the way he'd choose
    to go.

THE ELOCUTION LESSON

'Feel me breathe, girls,' –
Miss Bannerman places
Our pink open hands
On her emerald dress.

She presses our palms
Across thick, crinkly wool,
Our fingers extend
Along muscles and ribs.

'In – Out, In – Out,'
Miss Bannerman breathes,
Her bony chest heaves,
In – Out go our hands.

Our hands are pink fans
That Miss Bannerman breathes
Into movement, *In – Out*,
By the strength of her ribs.

Miss Bannerman's hair
Is a bright wavy brown,
Her lips are bright red,
Her body bright green,

Her eyes dark and sad,
Her thin ribs alive –
One by one, we draw back
While Miss Bannerman breathes.

THE SKELETON DANCE

We went to the pictures one bright afternoon,
There were serials, slapstick, and then a cartoon
Of skeletons dancing. That night I was soon
Woken up by the skeleton dance.

Those skeletons jiggled their fingers and toes
And juggled their thigh bones and skulls with no nose,
They grinned as their eye sockets gaped, and I froze
At the clattering skeletons' dance.

I ran to my mother and shook her awake –
'It's those skeletons dancing!' 'Those what? For my sake
Get back to your bed, it's past midnight, why make
Such a fuss for a skeleton dance!'

I said I was sorry, I pushed back her hair
To kiss her smooth forehead, now shining and bare,
And saw that her skin hid a skull. Even here
Was a skeleton waiting to dance.

Since that night long ago I have tried not to see
Her forehead – or yours – for it's bound to show me
The bone just below, which is waiting to be
Whirled away in the skeleton dance.

HYMN-SINGING IN SUFFOLK

We sat on the Green in the summertime sun
While the band was playing, the birds were singing,
We sat on the grass or lay in the shade
And sometimes we joined in the song.

The band was playing our favourite hymns,
We sat on the grass and we sang with the band,
The children raced like lambs in the sun
And then they slept in the shade.

The band in their uniforms stood in the sun,
Scarlet-faced, they played in the sun.
The leafy trees were as tall as the clouds
And most of us lay in the shade.

We lay on the grass and we drank lemonade,
We drank lemonade as we sang in the shade,
The band played our hymns in the summertime sun
So we gave them our lemonade.

The trees on the Green were as tall as the clouds,
The band kept playing, the birds kept singing,
The bandsmen played us our favourite hymns
And all of us joined in the song.

46 NURSING HOMES

THE SOCIAL WORKER

The news for you, the young man said,
Is that you have to find
A nursing home within a week.
I hope that's not unkind.
Our hospital has no more beds,
There's no more room: and so
Your mother with her mended hip,
Unmended mind, must go.

I have a list that you can take
With numbers you may ring
And what the cost will be. I think
That covers everything.
It's up to you. I've work to do.
No time to lose. And so
Remember, you have just one week.
Your mother has to go.

THE VERY FIRST SISTER

The very first Sister, so warm in her greeting,
Navy-blue, belted and bosomy. – Why
Is she packing up boxes? Dismayed at our greeting?
'Make yourself comfy,' says Sister. I sigh.
      'Never mind, never mind, never mind.
      It's your very first Home? Never fear.
      We'll care for your dear loved one here.
      Never mind. Never mind.'

'You've come to the right place, the best place, your worries
And troubles are over, so cheer up. You'll see
Our family home with its best rooms.' She hurries
Past boxes and suitcases. 'Then we'll have tea.
      Come with me, come with me, come with me.'
      She opens the very first door
      To a crowded room, silent, bare floor.
      'Come with me. Come with me.'

Kind-hearted Sister is kneeling and talking
To each nodding resident, to the young nurse
Who reads in the lamplight. Quick, Sister is walking
Busily onward. The next room is worse.
      'How are you? How are you? How are you?'
      She shouts to a dozen old men
      Who stand like grey ghosts. 'Cheer up then!
      Come on lads! How are you?'

'That was the dining-room. Now – ' Sister bustles
Down a long corridor, 'our Private Wing.'
She opens a door on more silence, no rustles
Of movement or breathing. 'Why didn't you ring?
      Mrs. Clark? Mrs. Clark? Mrs. Clark?
      You mustn't sit here in the dark.
      Just call, please cheer up, Mrs. Clark.
      Mrs. Clark? Mrs. Clark?'

We're back in the office with teacups and packing.
But where are the best rooms? We saw them? Then no,
No loved or unloved can come here. 'What is lacking?
It's really so bad then?' I can't cheer, I go.
      Time to go, time to go, time to go.
      Kind Sister who's worked here for years
      Kneels down to her packing in tears.
      Time to go. Time to go.

THE PRISONER UPSTAIRS

Drizzling weather. Here's the second recommended
    nursing home
Towering through evergreens.
Gravel drive, stone steps, a bell-pull. Echoes. Far off
    footsteps come.

Panelled hall with shining floorboards, twilit stairwell,
    gleaming stairs
Mounting up to galleries.
Each door numbered. Here's a nursery? Firelit, fuggy,
    beds, armchairs.

Bundled bodies doze in comfort, helpers carry cups of tea.
One cup goes behind a screen.
Here's a lady writing letters at her desk. She's glad to see

Someone fresh. She shows her window, open to the
    dripping rain,
Trees and fields and chilly air.
Landscape. She has books and photos. Home. She can't
    go out again.

Sticks and walking-frame have chained her. There's no lift.
    'But there's no harm
Stuck up here with these poor babes.'
Only, how they hate her window, blame her when they
    can't keep warm.

Breezes blow across her letters. Someone's hand has moved
    her screen.
Bedtime. Shut the window please.
So, goodnight across the stuffy tucked-up dreaming
    nursery scene.

Now the dark and glassy landing, stairwell, banisters to grip
Down the steep cascading stairs.
Next, the waxy glistening hallway, chairs to knock and
        mats that trip.

Last, the heavy front door, bolted. Six stone steps, no rail,
        no light –
Count them, slowly, nearly there.
Gravel drive, gate, street and freedom. Freedom, walking
        in the night.

THE NICEST HOME

A city set on a hill cannot be hid:
Which explains what we did:

We built our crystal palace,
Our pleasure dome, our bowl, inverted chalice,
High on the steepest hill
With our best skill –
Glass walls, glazed chintz, the kindest staff – until
The nicest people, with kin nicely ill
Drove in their powerful cars right up our hill
To share our view.

But this is not for you.

We don't have patients who could cause us trouble
Within our precious bubble,
Nor muddled folk inclined sometimes to wander
Beyond our splendour,
Nor anyone in any way unpleasant
(Unfair to those nice people here at present).

Who wouldn't like to laze in peacock chairs,
To gaze through glassy walls at whirling airs
And chilly clouds while they are safe and warm
And cared for kindly in our hilltop home?

THE HORSE

Someone sits at the top of the stairs,
Waiting for someone to come.
They promised her friendship and company,
Craftwork and cooking, a library,
Outings and art and activity.
She waits for someone to come.

Two people sit at the end of a room.
One of them reads a book.
She reads aloud with remembered care
To a blind old lady who sleeps in her chair
And a crowd of people who are not there,
Just emptiness and her book.

Soon, they say, we'll have cats and dogs,
We might even have a horse.
Soon there'll be residents, visitors, throng
Of experts, an exercise class, a sing-song.
Soon, they say, you'll feel you belong.
Soon you may feed the horse.

OUR TOUR OF LOCAL HOMES

On Saturday morning we drove to a hospital,
Kind to old people without too much capital –
Four storeys up and no garden – impractical.
Nobody offered us tea.

Then we hastened through lanes to a place recommended
By all the best experts (though this we amended),
'So sorry we're closed!' said a voice, and we ended
With Soup of the Day at The Lamb.

Next we rushed helter-skelter straight back to the city
To visit a Convent, the real nitty-gritty,
So shabby, so happy, so full. What a pity.
We treated ourselves to Mars Bars.

On Monday we breakfasted early and went
To three jolly widows who cheerfully spent
Their lives in one room (which was full), and this meant
There was just time for coffee and cake.

The worst place we saw was both crowded and smelly,
Everyone squeezed in their chairs watching telly,
Some pasty and scrawny, some flabby as jelly,
With one weary youngster in charge.

A run-down old mansion had staff who were fonder
Of elderly people and let them all wander
Or help or behave as they liked, which we ponder.
(On Wednesday we dined at The Dog.)

On Thursday, exhausted, we thought we had found
The right place at last. Full of course. 'You two sound,'
Said the motherly lady who'd shown us around,
'As if you should join us for tea.'

THE CHOICE

How shall we choose our Home? This one so dark,
Another stately, pillared hall and park.
The next is bare and chilly, that one small,
Here stairs are steep, and here no lift at all.
The Mount (we saw last week) was vast and gloomy,
The Cedars plush – a grand hotel, and roomy
(Which scared our mother off). The Grange serves sherry,
The floors aren't swept, the residents are merry,
It should have been our choice, shabby and kind.
Our worst mistake. – The Glebe was hard to find,
The Sister snappy. We were glad to go
And see The Willow Tree. Superb. But no,
We're not superb ourselves. They want the best.
We also fail The Lansdowne's sterner test
Where all play bridge all day in tweeds and pearls.
But sloppy Studland? Sulky, sullen girls
Complain to us, the place is being sold.
Here, there are only beds, no chairs. There, gold
Paid on the nail would last six weeks. – We're weary
Of all this driving. Fontwell's cheap, but dreary.
The Homes that seem just right are always full
Or far too far – more travelling. Some pull
Our heartstrings. Forty homes, and most refuse
Imperfect elderly. We beg. They choose.

A STORY

Welcome! A story!
(Words pour like pebbles rushing
Over a clifftop.)

Yesterday morning
(Words blaze and change in falling),
Such an adventure!

She made her escape,
She pulled high bolts with a stick,
She ran miles and miles

But then, someone kind.
Such fuss, such end of freedom. –
Well told, old lady.

THE CHAIR BY THE DOOR

Edward sat by the door.
Such a gentleman, Edward.
He sat in that chair by the door,
But now Edward has gone.

Arthur never sat there.
Louise though, she sat by the door,
Nodding and laughing, Louise.
Louise also has gone.

Arthur was really quite young,
He used to keep on about pain,
Some pain in his stomach, he said,
And Arthur was suddenly gone

Without any time by the door.
Pearl liked him. Pearl sits by the door.
They've dressed Pearl in Betty's clothes,
So Pearl is sure to be gone.

THE CARE ASSISTANT

Each day I say my name.
Each day it's just the same.
At first it seemed a game.

I never thought it true,
Each day they think I'm new,
They ask me, 'Who are you?'

I wish it were a game.
They ask and ask my name.
It doesn't sound the same.

They're old, and glad I'm new
And pretty. 'Who are you?'
They ask, but I'm not true,

I'm strange, I'm not the same.
My name sounds like their game.
Each day I say my name.

THE WAITING LIST

Summer again,
And I have come
To our last home
Down a leafy lane
At the edge of the town
Where children play
In the setting sun,
In its blinding ray.

A family home
Where the owners frown,
They will put our name down
But they have no room,
Just a waiting list.
Sometimes beds become free.
If I insist
I am welcome to see.

Dogs bark in the hall,
The husband stands
With a plate in his hands
While his children call
And his wife and I
Climb flights of stairs
To a room full of sky
Which a friend thinks hers.

A hospital pays
For the next room where
Two people stare.
The owner says
There is one more room
Where a vacancy
Could occur soon.
Would I like to see?

The room is small,
Silent, bare,
A table and chair,
A bed by the wall,
A window above
Crowded by trees.
Dark leaves move
In the evening breeze

And shadow and speckle
Bed and chair,
Shift everywhere,
Mottle, freckle,
Flicker and fade
On walls and floor.
My hand becomes shade
As I shut the door.

I kneel on the bed,
Look out at flowers,
This view could be ours,
Trees overhead
Could be lopped to allow
More light, more air,
But not just now,
There is someone here.

A freckled hand
Lies beside mine
And moves as a sign.
I understand
That this bed isn't free,
We must wait on the list,
Though our vacancy
May soon exist.

A WONDERFUL VIEW OF THE SEA

The visitors say
    Such a wonderful view from her very own window of
    golf-links and marshes and blue in the summertime sea
And they add
    The food looks quite nice and even smells nice but we've
    travelled such miles that we really would like some hot tea
Also
    She has all that she needs such as magazines newspapers
    radio TV and telephone right by her bed
Furthermore
    She has *en suite* facilities (bathroom and toilet) and bell for
    emergencies Staff Room next door to her – we've all said
How we wish we could be here instead.

The resident says
    Since my spectacles broke and got lost and my
                    cataracts grew,
                    What use is a view?
    Since my false teeth were dropped down the drain and
                    were washed out to sea,
                    Food's been hard work for me,
    Since my deaf aids keep whistling, my fingers can't
                    fit them, they fall,
                    I don't hear you at all.
    Since the nurses won't come and the toilet's too far and
                    I'm blamed,
                    I feel so ashamed.
    The world and its interests and pleasures are all
                    leaving me.
                    Is it too hard to see

That I'm bored, I've become such a fool and I wish
I could die.
I'm sorry. Goodbye.

The staff say

She gave us a lot of trouble,
She used to get very low,
But she was an old dear really,
We're sorry she had to go.

NOTES

Page

9   AMERICAN FRIENDS
     The friends were American: the location was New York City.

29   'PENALTY KICK FOR PARKING ON YELLOW LINE'
     Taken from three articles in the *Observer*, dated 20 September, 27
     September and 4 October 1987.

36   CRESSEID BLAMES THE GODS
     Cresseid has several names and identities, having been the acci-
     dental creation of various medieval story-tellers. This Cresseid is
     from Robert Henryson's *Testament of Cresseid*. The last stanza is
     from an advertisement aimed at raising funds for the treatment of
     leprosy.

39   BRUGES
     The 'thrice consumed belfry' comes from the opening stanza of a
     poem by Henry Longfellow:

> In the market place of Bruges stands the
>   belfry old and brown;
> Thrice consumed and thrice rebuilded, still
>   it watches o'er the town.

49   THE ROOM IN THE TOWER
     Only one in a terrifying book of ghost stories by E. F. Benson – all
     these stories could do with exorcism.

58   SOMETHING OF HIMSELF
     Rudyard Kipling's autobiography, *Something of Myself*, contains
     little of himself or of his family and seems mainly to be written as
     the public record of a successful writer. The few pages on the
     House of Desolation end with the conclusion that 'In the long run
     these things . . . drained me of any capacity for real, personal hate
     for the rest of my days.' He mentions the birth of his children but
     gives no further information such as the death of his son in the
     Great War. So I have used his public poem 'The Beginnings' to
     carry the something more of himself that drives this poem and

two of his stories – 'Baa Baa Black Sheep' and 'Mary Postgate' (Mary Postgate being a respectable middle-aged woman who murdered a German airman in revenge).

60–1   STORIES OF CHINA and PARENTS
Both these poems are about our parents' and my sister's experiences in China and on the journey home. Trebitsch Lincoln, an international spy, appears as the new nurse at the end of 'Stories of China', and as my sister's baby-sitter in 'Parents'. He was travelling by sea from China to England, where his son was to be hanged for murder. Because of his reputation as a spy, he was forbidden to go ashore at any port. When the ship reached England he was forbidden to land and so could not say good-bye to his son. He was using an assumed name and claimed to be a doctor, and our parents therefore trusted him to mind their baby daughter. We have a photograph of him, a portly gentleman dressed in white.

71ff   46 NURSING HOMES
Strictly speaking, there is a distinction between Nursing Homes, Rest Homes etc.

New and Recent Poetry from Anvil

TONY CONNOR
Metamorphic Adventures

CAROL ANN DUFFY (ed.)
Anvil New Poets 2

PETER DALE
Edge to Edge
NEW AND SELECTED POEMS

DICK DAVIS
Touchwood

MICHAEL HAMBURGER
Collected Poems 1941–1994

JAMES HARPUR
The Monk's Dream

ANTHONY HOWELL
First Time in Japan

PETER LEVI
Reed Music

E. A. MARKHAM
Misapprehensions

THOMAS McCARTHY
The Lost Province

PETER RUSSELL
The Elegies of Quintilius

PHILIP SHERRARD
In the Sign of the Rainbow
SELECTED POEMS 1940–1989

A catalogue of our publications is available on request